Patricia Davis

Mending Me...
The Unscripted Route

Wider Perspectives Publishing ∞ 2023 ∞ Norfolk, Va. ∞ 2021

Copyright © September 2023, Patricia Davis, writing as *Patricia*
Wider Perspectives Publishing, Norfolk, Va
ISBN: 978-1-952773-82-2

Mending Me
:The Unscripted Route

With God all things are possible.

Finding solace in the journey of healing. I thought healing was planned and could be contributed to a certain amount of time. Turns out the healing was up to me and only me. Time nor space can be a determining factor.

At the start of my writing in September 2021, I was lost. I felt alone and most often wanting nothing to do with the life I was currently living. I thought anger, resentment and even suicide would be the best answer for the many problems I was facing. I blamed everyone I could except me. The life I was living was the life I created regardless of whether or not I wanted it.

I had a pivotal moment in my life in May of 2021 where I realized I was the source. I was source of everything I was experiencing. I also came to realization that I was the only one who could change it. Prayers make a difference, but not if you don't have the faith to go along with them. It's almost like releasing helium filled balloons into the sky, hoping they reach the stars above. Sadly, they never do and eventually fall back to the ground.

I took several steps to make changes in my life, one being my education. I decided to go back to school to pursue my bachelors in contemplative psychology. Although this field was way off my radar of things I wanted to accomplish, I knew I needed help. But I didn't really want anyone to help me, per say; like therapy or counseling. So I decided to study psychology to help heal myself.

Upon the start of my classes, I noticed that a lot of my assignments could be turned in as poetry. I haven't written poetry in years and had no where to start. I began googling poetry in the 757 and found a few open mics. The one open mic that kept popping up was The Venue on 35th street. A couple of weeks passed and I decided to make the trip on a Monday night to get some inspiration for my studies. I found so much more there that it's quite hard to explain.

I remember the first open mic I went to, and the performances were outstanding. I don't really remember the talents, per say, but something that stood out to me were the people. They seemed so comfortable in the spaces that they held, however that may look and express itself. I found home far far away from home.

This has been the start to my writing, although I've been writing all along. I'm learning my voice not just physical, but mental, emotional and spiritual. I'm learning who I am in the darkest of times and also the brightest of times.

Everyday is such an adventure that I now look forward to experiencing. The many experiences each day allow for a new perspective, a new canvas and a new meaning. These pieces are a collection of my revelations on this healing journey that I now know is a lifelong process. One that I look forward to encountering.

In Jesus' name.

Dedication

Mom
Dad
Leah, Shaun III
Shaun Jr.
Peter Jr.

Acknowledgment

Thank you, God, for guiding me to the Venue on 35th.
The place it holds in my heart is beyond words, beyond truth.

Contents

Mending Deserves Acknowledgment

I

Starting with broken pieces...

Note to Self

I'm sorry.
I'm sorry I didn't listen to you.
I'm sorry I didn't take the time to hear even one syllable that rolled
off your tongue.

You.
Yes you,
black child.
I'm sorry.

I was afraid of how I might be seen.
Afraid of how I might feel.
I was afraid to listen to my own cries.

To know the struggles
of the people before me,
made me uncomfortable.

I didn't want to know why they were so angry.
I didn't care to even allow my mind to empathize.

I believed that they were bitter.
I thought they were angry
and would take a chance to hurt anyone they could!

As a child,
I received distinct views on blacks
which implanted their way into my mind.

I believed in what I was told.

How,
dark skin was ugly but then told me I'm beautiful.
How,
Ghetto blacks were but told me I'm well behaved.
How,
Horribly blacks communicated then told me,
I talked "white."

I'm sorry,
Black women.

Truth is I envied you.

I envied you because of how you presented yourself.
You seemed so free in a world where I wanted to be.
You seemed to know exactly how you felt
and had no problem saying it.

It made me feel weak.

For most of my childhood,
I tried to be everything other than black,
(whatever the hell that is).

I'm sorry,
Patricia.

I'm sorry,
I neglected you.

I'm sorry,
I never acknowledged you.

Mending Me...

Patricia

I'm sorry,
I erased you.

Forgive me.

Prayer Ingredients

I was taught.
Learn your ABCs
and 123s

Learn when you shouldn't.
You couldn't get me to teach.
To preach.

However,
This requires a sit down.

I've learned prayers get me to and through.

Be careful what you ask for.

I asked for tranquility,
But You took her.

You broke me.
Showed me my prayers are for the weak.

I prayed your healing hands,
would take the pain God.
Take,
This Pain God!

Prayers make requests for meals without ingredients.
Dispensed right where I can reach them.
I'm sold.

Mending Me...

Asking for such things,
I knew not what to do with.

A mixture of what I thought I needed,
And what you required.

I'm praying like I was taught.
No.
Pray for direction.
Correction in my inflection,
Pray for meetings.
Pray for time spent.
Pray on purpose.

Self Worth

Mama ain't raise no fool,
But
Mama warned me.

"Patricia,
Them bullies at school not nice.

They will say mean things to ya.
Make you feel real bad,
but don't listen to em.

They're just opinions.
They're just words."

Woven into thread,
sewed with precision.

Stitch,
By stitch.

They hurt.

Nobody told me what to do,
When the real bully seems to be me.

Often my thoughts take the stage.
They be right here.

And I'm front row seat!

Mending Me...

Before someone compliments you,
degrade yourself.

Before you put that on,
It
does not
work.

Before you think you're beautiful,
I'll make you think,
every mole on your face
was strategically placed
in the opposition of self worth.

That's right!
Where's your worth at baby girl!

How come they only teach you to fight
with words and fists?

Love thyself.

Mama said if someone isn't nice to you,
tell the teacher.

Okay.

So,
Who do I tell now?

Daddy's Love is Just Enough
:15 August 2022

If daddy loved a child like me,
he'd issue hugs.

Usher me on the inside,
Church.
He'd clap with me in,
church.

Resentment,
Submerged.

Baptisms cleanse,
Remember?

Yesterdays sermon doesn't linger past dawn.
Daddy I'm home!

Cigarettes and Seagram's fill the air like,
fresh breath kisses.
I love you.

Daddy,
As I grace your presence
my smiles,
hide home in you.

You've made room for me!
Like an open pew
at the very front of the church!

Mending Me...

Patricia

Your stance,
abolishes my fears.
You show up now,
better than ever before!

My smile,
conceals your slurred speech
And staggered steps.

Daddy, adores my smiles!

Today's sermon is about remission.
(Ephesians 4:22)

And how,
nothing ever comes how we want it.
But how we need it.
(2 Corinthians 12:9)

Daddy chose me.
Just like,
me chose daddy.
Like,
love chose my daddy.

His love is,
just enough.

What is Black?

Black.
Never really felt too black.
Just like,
real black.

How in the summer time,
my skin turns to a shade
only the palest of pales could imagine.

I watch as it bends with sunlight.
Dances with my tears.
And acts up in fear.

Black.
Never really felt too black.
Just like,
that.

I've always been a fan of the color.
Yous too black.

Black.
I don't know all the cool songs,
And to be honest I'm not a fan of his-story.

Black.
I do know I'm here.

As my complexion sprouts from within
Sneak peaks..
See?

Mending Me...

Patricia

Black.
I just know I'm free.
Not because you told me,
But because I am this.
See?

Chaos

Chaos.

My children's room at 4pm sharp everyday.
If I step on another tiny monster truck,
I'll need ankle surgery.

Parental chaos.

The crowds during a concert
of an artist my friend invited me to.
I don't know the artist.
I don't know the songs.
Everyone is singing.

Mental chaos.

The overwhelming desire to explain myself.
In the hopes that someone,
will just listen.
And the realization,
that no one ever truly just listens.
Cause everyone has the answer.

Self sabotaging chaos.

Acting clueless on purpose.
It's not that I don't understand,
it just takes me longer,
So the joke IS funny,
just later.

Mending Me...

Comedic chaos.

I ran up a hill the other day,
only to find that indeed
I had to get down that same hill.

Physical chaos.

If you notice me just a tad bit more,
you'll notice I'm nothing like before.

The evolution of my chaos.

Farewell

Well,
this is my letter
Goodbye.

So long
you.

You've fought beyond measure.

You build bridges over barriers
with ease.

Picked up my slack.
Stood for something.

A test,
To natures dynamics.

You mean well.
You mean,
Well.

Mending Me...

Exposure

Facing you

When I stand
here, do you see me?

I think you,
I think you see my weakness.

My darkest secrets,
And my biggest mistakes.

You see my cuts,
bruises,
And scars.

Wardrobe changes
Are my master facade.

Feel Feel

Writing gives me a chance to feel.

Cope.

Hope.

Tomorrow is just today,

Concealed.

Patricia

II

Brokenness mends with love.

Mending Me...

Reflections

Within me.

Purely guarded,
hopeful.

Within you.

Molded forms of me.
Gentle I see.

Searched

Dark skin,
fits right in.

Not meshed with weakness.

Sold not soiled,
leads to
The Answer.

Sweet Power of Hymn

If I knew my time was limited,
I'd make better choices.

I'd want,
in ways deserving of an Oscar.

Singing to me.

Amazing grace.
Sweet sounds.

Music makes me smile.
It makes my heart open with clarity
I become human,
Again.
You become human,
Again.

Home

Trust feels like
lonely nights,
In the dome.

Just before sunset.

O,
how the powers that be,
Make it a sight to see.

At last,
Alone.

Enough

Often,
I like to write from different perspectives.
They're all me,
But not really.

I enjoy the sound of the birds
when I first wake up.
Yellow flashes of tweets,
Tucked just under Gods sheets.

I wonder what it must feel like to be here.
Is it rainbows and stuff?

Just enough,
I suppose.

I concern myself often,
with how much I think.

So actually,
I'll never write a long piece.

That's like converging
And packing down,
50 11 seats.

I believe that whoever I'm trying to be
Is just a hairline away.

From being smacked by an 18 wheeler,
On the free way.

I feel so connected
to absolutely nothing.

Nothing makes sense.

Because how does expression,
result in the tale of two tales.

That's just forbidden Pretense.

Often,
I like to write from different perspectives.
They're all me,
But not really.

The Meat

Purpose cannot stand within reason.

Nor can it be challenged.

As much you stray,

It must continuously locate it's prey.

Bring the Energy

I am always the energy.

The energy,
that is first used to guide a greeting.

You feed off my presence.
Hunger.

I bring the hue of ease.
Comfort.

This makes me your need.
Necessity.

Begging for a dose.
Please.

Mending Me

Just, 10 Things I Desire

1. Put God First.
2. Justice. Not punishment rather, just walk a mile in my shoes. See me how I see you. I love you.
3. Settle less. Do what you can, when you can. Do nothing, when you can't. Your worth reigns.
4. Be love. Be a place of healing and therapeutic reckoning for everyone you encounter. Love them. Let the space become insignificant. Be love.
5. Trust you. She has been with you this whole way. What more can she prove!?
6. Remember limitless always wins. Free yourself, from the confines of your insecurities.
7. Give more than you receive Patricia. Nothing can come with.
8. The wisdom to resonate with life. Its ups, downs, the short comings, the falls, the rolls, the joys, the moments I'll never get back and the people, I'll never get back.
9. Break through. Step into each day knowing the only barriers before me, are the barriers placed them. I allowed them. I allowed them. I allowed them. For I figured it'd be easier stay beneath them.
10. Put. God. Here.

III

Mending deserves

acknowledgment.

All the Things I Expected of You

I expected too damn much.

I Trusted you to support me.

To mold me,
into the woman that graces entrances without hesitation.

To love me greater than I loved myself

To guide my tears away from sadness

To correct my anger with pleasure

To embrace my presence like the very first meeting

To highlight my waking hours with constant reassurance that this
will never end

To fight for an infinite experience with you

To fight like the end is a losing battle
You desperately strove to escape

To fight,
To never,
Let this end.

Self Analysis

I just want you to know I love you.

It's what I tell you not often enough.
I don't repeat it when I should.

I don't remember,
to repeat it often enough.

But When I say I love you,
I can't really,
love you.

Because,
I don't know you.

You're encased in some vessel that looks
nothing like what I imagined you to be.

I imagined your voice higher.
I imagined your height,
Just a lil' bit taller.

I imagined your smile to feel exactly how it looks.
But,
When I look at you in the mirror,
you
Look
Different.

Mending Me...

Life.

I imagined your life would play out differently.

You'd be some doctor,
looking in women's vaginas and
going out for mimosas on the weekends.

You'd be reading books under a dim lamp.
And wearing heels that never hurt your feet.
But you don't even like heels.

Imagination will have you thinking that you shouldn't be here.
You should be somewhere that you fixate your mind to, so that
your current situation doesn't remind of your stagnant present.

Whole time I'm imaging what I wanted,
God's plan had already started.

Less Trying

If you listen really close,
You can hear the bullshit a mile away.

Smells like piss,
And walks like a snail.

Trails become clues,
That lead to candor.

Uncircumcised once
On the path to liberation.

Helpless although persuasive in meaning.

None like you.

Spoken For

Truth speaks in many ways.
Through deceptive eyes
And teeth that smile.

Fond memories of you,
Spewing from underneath your garments.

On the darkest of days,
Truth speaks with the dimmest light.

Speaking from uncertainty,
Because nothing is ever certain.

Speaking when no asked,
Because it restores your pride.

Speaking with piercing joy,
As sharpened knives.

Become comrades with enemies.
Compassion kills malice at its interior.

Yet, Truth speaks most prominent in to you.

She's Me

Black Petals need roses
Unbound and Free
No more life to be

She's me.

Petals dusted in compliments
And just the right amount of love.

Because roses smell,
like love.

I thought about this moment,
Death is evident.

They say to care for a rose you must pick the right location.
Locations cause manifestations.
Thank you God.

Then, You water.
Roses need water,
Too.

And finally
Pruning which technically means
The removal or reduction of parts of a plant that serve no purpose
Let it go.

Black Petals need roses
Unbound and free
No more life to be

She's me.

Dark Place

I'm in an extremely dark place.

Being here is tolerable.
Being here is needed.
Being here,
it's still safe.

Indication,
This helps me grow.
Expansion.

I acknowledge,
that I am here.

Dark days don't always consume light.
Voices creep.

Without today,
Grace is referred to as,
Colorless sunsets.

Distance reflects pain as mirages.
Time displaces,
True light.

So Me

So Me.

You've misspoken.

You seek in others what comforts you most.
You liar..
I admire this attire.

You feel for fun.
You're out on display ever chance you get.

You stab,
No take backs.

You cheat for thrill.

Tell it from the other side,
You're confused.

Ladies and gentlemen this is just a drill.
You're welcome.

A Different Now

I love now.

This time feels different.
Framed just for my eye to see,
Take a peak.

This is different.

I woke up confused,
how my cravings turned into prayers.

Why,
My tongue began phrases with
I love you and not Bitch.

Why,
I only want to see you smile
even after the pain.

Chile,
This isn't war.
It's my freedom!

I was waiting to forget you.
I waited for you to come back.
I waited for my wounds to heal like magic.
You,
waved goodbye.

But see,
this time
its different.

Crumbs

Like wind,
I can never see.

The pain I have buried beneath me.

Fear.

Trust your crumbs.
Little gems you've left along the way.

Useful Tools.

So, I see what I'm doing here.
I start a poem and never finish it.
But,
I Believe it.
I Breathe it.

Till,
It no longer consoles me.

The water don't flow no more.
The birds don't fly no more.
The fish just don't swim no more.

Here.
Are just a few crumbs.

Mending Me...

Unspoken

:6 March 2023

With Gratitude God,

Thank you for the words unspoken.
My mind is your canvas.
Speak to me in ways
My eyes yearn to know.

Thank you for your grace upon my life.
You stand beside me through.
The secrets,
 I cannot fathom
laying on desired ears.

Thank you for my posture.
When in and through me,
You are my rod.
This body May ache,
But you heal through intention.

Thank you God for this day.
One I hold true to my heart.
I balance these halls,
As I balance these steps.
Steps they say,
Thousands desire to see.
But.

Thank you For moving me.
For dancing with me while
I show forth my commitment to you Father.

Thank you for your persuasive Essence.
Guiding me through maturity with wings,
Cast on this road,
Unspoken.

Mending Me...

end

... Mend Me

Mom Mends

Mom Mends is dedicated to providing nurturing environments where mothers can find healing, empowerment, and personal growth. The organization's primary goal is to help mothers rediscover self-love and self-awareness, fostering their individual healing and success. By emphasizing these aspects, Mom Mends aims to enhance overall parenting success, creating a positive impact on both mothers and their families.

Patricia

<u>colophon</u>
Brought to you by Wider Perspectives Publishing, care of James Wilson, with the mission of advancing the poetry and creative community of Hampton Roads, Virginia.
See our production of works from ...

Serena Fusek
Chichi Iwuorie
Symay Rhodes
Terra Leigh
Samantha Borders-Shoemaker
J. Scott Wilson (TEECH!)
Charles Wilson
Gloria Darlene Mann
Neil Spirtas
Jorge Mendez & JT Williams
Sarah Eileen Williams
Stephanie Diana (Noftz)
* the Hampton Roads
            Artistic Collective
Jason Brown (Drk Mtr)
Martina Champion
Ken Sutton

Crickyt J. Expression
Cassandra IsFree
Nich (Nicholis Williams)
Samantha Geovjian Clarke
Natalie Morison-Uzzle
Gus Woodward II
Patsy Bickerstaff
Taz Wetsweete'
Jack Cassada
Dezz
Catherine TL Hodges
Kent Knowlton
Linda Spence-Howard
Tony Broadway
Zach Crowe
... and others to come soon.

We promote and support the artists of the 757
from the seats, from the stands,
from the snapping fingers and clapping hands
from the pages, and the stages
and now we pass them forth
to the ages

Check for the above artists on
FaceBook, the Virginia Poetry
Online channel on YouTube,
    and other social media.

* Hampton Roads Artistic Collective is an extension of WPP which strives to simultaneously support worthy causes in Hampton Roads and the local creative artists.

44

Made in the USA
Middletown, DE
19 January 2024